FIVE WALLABIES and ONE DOG NIGHT

FAY NELSON

Ordering Information:

Prime Seven Media
518 Landmann St.
Tomah City, WI 54660

Printed in the United States of America

Hello, my name is Rufus.

I live on a farm in the bush with my Mum, my brothers Bunjee and Poly, and my sister Molly Dolly. Mum is a person, but she is my Mum, really, because she loves me and she gives me lots of cuddles. My real Mum, is a lovely little Pomeranian dog, who I left when I was six weeks old, to go and live with my 'person Mum'.

Bunjee and Poly were already on the farm when I came. They are my brothers, even though they are Jack Russell dogs, I love them. Poly is thirteen years old, so he is an elder dog. Sometimes he is a grump and he tells Bunjee and me what to do – but I don't do what he tells me to do.

Poly's name is really Napoleon, but we call him 'Poly'. Bunjee's name is from Mum's language. She is of the Bandjin people, an Aboriginal group who once lived on an island, and Bunjee means 'Mate' in Mum's language.

Molly Dolly, was also on the farm when I came. She is my sister, even though she is a cat, and I love her too.

After helping Mum in the garden, we went into the backyard to have afternoon tea with her. We love that time because Mum gives us our biscuits. Sometimes she brushes our hair and gives us cuddles.

After afternoon tea, Mum and I went inside so she could make her dinner. Mum always listens to the radio and the news – she said it was important to know what people who live in other places are doing.

I fell asleep, then Mum called out to me, "Rufus wake up, come quickly, we have to help someone."

I rubbed my eyes and ran to the door that Mum was holding open for me. She closed it behind me to keep the snakes out. "Bunjee, Poly," Mum called out. The boys scrambled to get out of their kennels – they knew Mum was upset by the sound of her voice.

Mum kneeled down in front of us and said, "boys listen to me, we have to help find Bina the little girl who lives on the farm up the road. I heard her Mummy on the radio saying Bina is lost in the bush, and she is asking people to come and search the bush for her.

"So, we will go and find her footprints and the smell of her little body. We have to find her quickly before the night comes, and that will be soon.

"Boys, we have to make sure she is not near the river or the dams – she is a little girl, who does not understand the danger if she goes into the water.

"We will go different ways." She put her hand under Bunjee's jaw and kissed the top of his head. She looked him in the eyes and said, "Bunjee, you are the faster runner, so you will look for Bina along both sides of the river.

"If you find her scent, howl out loud to tell us where you are."

Bunjee started to run away but stopped and ran back to Mum. He stood on his hind legs and slurped a sloppy kiss on her hand. Mum patted him on the head and said, "Mummy loves you too, Bunjee Boy, go quickly and find Bina, she needs you to keep her safe and warm.

"Poly, you will look around the two dams in the big paddock, and all the grassy spots, and the dam across the road – howl if you find Bina. You must cuddle her to keep her warm." Poly looked at Mum and me and barked twice before looking in the direction of the big paddock dams.

"Rufus, you and I will explore the hill paddock, and you will howl if we find her.

"Boys, you will ask all the birds and all the animals you see, to tell you where Bina is if they see her. We are all bush animals and bush people, we must work together to find her. Now go quickly."

We all ran to where Mum said for us to go. Bunjee and Poly and I had our noses to the ground running zig-zag everywhere, sniffing the ground to find if Bina had walked there.

Soon they were out of sight as Mum and I walked up the hill. I sniffed the ground and Mum called Bina's name, but she didn't answer. Mum said, "Rufus, I am worried about her, it is getting dark and the night will be cold. We have to go home."

As we walked, Poly came out of the long grass. I asked him if Bina had been in the big paddock and he said, "no." He then added, "I asked Melee Wallaby, Princess Echidna and Seesee Water Dragon Lizard – they said they had been all over the big paddock, while Tilla Chicken Hawk flew overhead, but no one saw her."

Just then we heard a noise. We looked around and saw Lipee and Momba Frill-Necked Lizards coming out of the long grass near the old tree with Witchu Wombat. Poly said to them, "did you see Bina and Bunjee?" They said, "yes, Bina was down near the old wattle tree. We said she should go home, but she just smiled and waved to us, and kept walking along the river bank."

Poly was sniffing the ground, running here and there. He started scratching the ground then he howled loudly and said, "Mum, Bina was here." He ran quickly following Bina's footprints and her scent. But he lost her scent because she crossed a shallow water-way.

We looked up into the trees and we saw Mrs Possum. She said she hadn't seen either Bina or Bunjee, as she had been sleeping and had just woken up.

The dark was settling in and Mum said, "we must go home boys, it is too dark for us to see. I might fall over and hurt myself and that would make matters worse." Mum was crying, so we knew we would have to look after her, and get her home safely.

I scratched Mum on the leg and looked towards the river, asking her where Bunjee was. We walked to the river bank and called out his name. Poly and I howled but he didn't answer.

There were tears in Mum's eyes and the tears ran down her cheeks. She was crying for Bina and Bunjee. Poly and I stood on our hind legs, our paws on Mum's legs. We were sad too. We were saying, "Mum don't cry, Bunjee will find her."

Mum patted both of us and said, "I am worried about Bunjee too."

We watched the sun go down behind our hill, and then the flying foxes filled the sky.

We heard the flapping of wings. They were so close to us.

Poly and I called to them to watch for Bina and Bunjee. They circled around and came above us and said, "yes we will, there are many of us. Some of us will fly up to the cave on the hill and talk with Manjuwi the Bush Spirit Man and his helper, Minimi.

"They see many things, because they can see all things from their cave that is high on the hill.

"We will fly along the river, because we can search in the dark. If they are there, we will find them.

"Go home and rest and wait for us to come."

We began walking home. Mum said, "boys, we have to ask the Spirits for their help tonight, for Bunjee and Bina's sake. We need everyone's help."

I looked up into a large dead tree and was surprised to see a mother flying fox and her baby. They were hanging upside down from the tree branch, and the mother had wrapped her wings around her baby to keep him warm, and to stop him falling from the tree.

Poly and I barked loudly at them, asking if they had seen Bina. "Boys," Mum said, "be good, please lower your voices and please call her 'Mrs Flying Fox'. That will be showing your good manners and respect for her. She is older than you and is all grown up with a baby." Poly and I lowered our heads and our tails to show Mum we understood, and were sorry we shouted at Mrs Flying Fox.

Mrs Flying Fox said, "thank you. We have been to see Manjuwi and Minimi up in their cave on the hill. Manjuwi said Bunjee is a very smart dog. He knows the bush and he will find Bina. They asked Melee Wallaby and her family to help find Bina, so all bush and water animals and birds will look for her, and when they find her, they will look after her."

"Thank you," we said. The baby looked at us and said, "I am happy that my Mummy wraps her wings around me, so I am with her always. I would cry if I was alone without my Mummy."

Poly and I looked up at Mrs Flying Fox. Poly tried to sit up to talk to her, but he fell over backwards. I said to Poly, "no wonder you fell over, Poly, you had such a big dinner, just look at your big tummy!"

We looked up at the cave on the hill. It was getting darker. The sun had almost gone to sleep behind the hill.

We could see three grass trees at the entrance to the cave, their long thin leaves hanged down peacefully, ready to go to sleep.

Manjuwi and Minimi appeared. Minimi waved to us. Mum saw them too. She looked at us and said softly, "let's go home boys."

With the darkness settling in, the cold air was beginning to settle on the ground. Maybe a frost would come tonight. That would be so cold for Bunjee and Bina.

Mum said, "we will go inside now. Come boys." Molly Dolly was waiting at the back door. She 'meowed' many times saying to us, "where is our brother Bunjee?" It was the first time our little family would go to bed with one of us missing.

Mum lit the fire and placed a blanket in front of it for Poly and me to lie on. We said, "Mum, don't worry about dinner for us, we are not hungry." Mum said, "OK, I know we are worried about Bunjee and Bina, I just hope Cary Carpet Snake is not looking for food tonight, and she stays in her warm nest."

We soon fell asleep, but we kept waking up because we missed Bunjee.

Bunjee was sniffing the ground when he found Bina's scent.

He saw leaves overturned where she had walked and saw she had even stumbled and fallen down. Bunjee had learned how to read the message of the overturned leaves from Mum's father, when he was asked by Police to find other people who had got lost in the bush.

He barked loudly four times, hoping Bina would say something or cry.

He didn't hear anything, so he barked again many times. When he stopped barking, he heard Bina crying. He ran to her. She was standing in the river. She looked so cold and she was shivering.

Then Bina fell over. Bunjee rushed to her. He placed his body closer to her, so she was able to put her arms around his neck. But Bunjee knew he had to get Bina out of the water, she was so cold she couldn't walk.

So, Bunjee took the sleeve of her shirt in his mouth and began to pull her out of the water. He then walked her back to the river bank to safety.

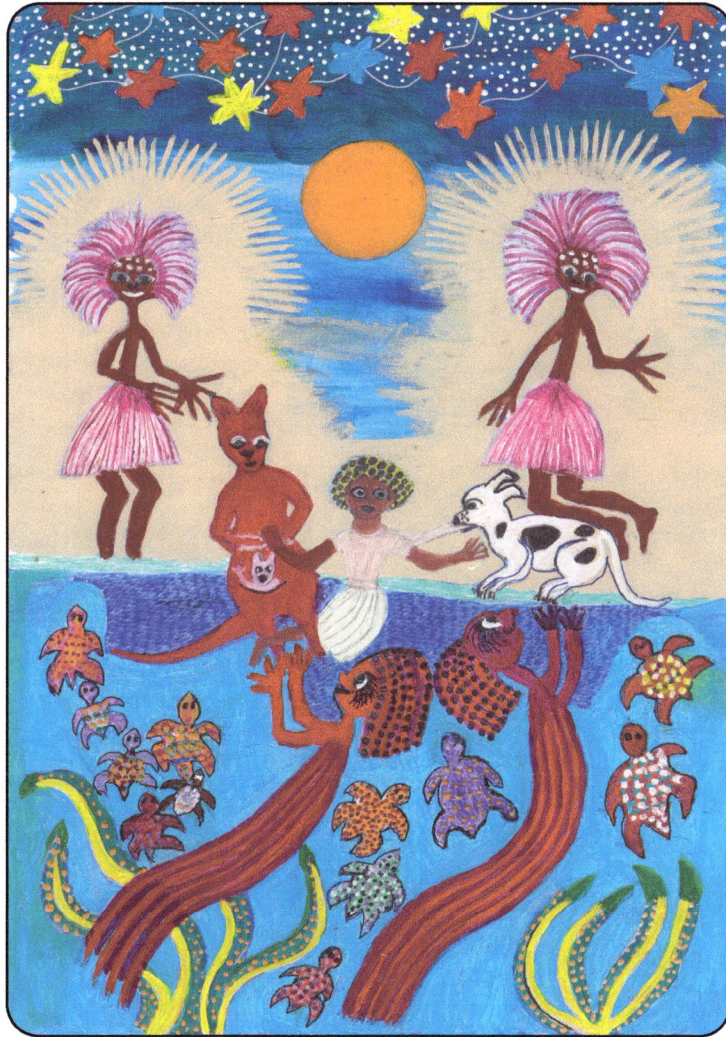

"Bunjee," Melee Wallaby said, "my family can keep Bina warm with our furry bodies." Melee Wallaby and her family were standing there very close to Bina. Melee Wallaby said, "Bunjee, we have to take Bina's wet clothes off her."

Bunjee said, "I can't do that, you have to do it, your paws are better than mine, they are like people's hands." Melee Wallaby said, "OK," and then added, "Bunjee, go up to that farm house and look in the shed. You will find blankets, they are old and dusty, but bring them to me."

Bunjee said, "we should try to take her home." Melee Wallaby said, "no, she is too cold, she cannot walk and she will freeze. We will take her wet clothes off, and our family will cuddle her with our bodies. Our fur will keep her warm until you come back with the blankets."

Bunjee ran off to the farm house. There were no lights on, the people were away. There were no lights on in the shed either, but Bunjee sniffed around in the dark. He found the blankets and took one in his mouth and began dragging it back to the river.

When he returned, the wallabies had cuddled around Bina so closely, all Bunjee could see was her head.

Melee Wallaby said, "Bina has stopped shivering. She can lie on the blanket, it is big enough to cover her and we will all lie very close to her, to keep her warm." Bunjee said, "me too, yes we are a 'five wallabies and one dog night' in Bina's little life."

The wallabies pulled the blanket over Bina and lay down very close to her. Bunjee found a space and lay down with them.

Bunjee looked up and saw two Bush Dreaming Spirits, Juma and Williya, watching him. They said, "Bunjee, you are a real hero, you saved Bina. We came to help you, but you didn't need our help at all."

Just then, two Water Dreaming Spirits, Martiama and Lillitja, popped up out of the water and said, "we are here to help too." Melee Wallaby said, "yes, I held Bina's legs so she didn't sink into the deep water." Tippy, Melee Wallaby's baby, who was in her mother's pouch, waved and said in her squeaky little voice, "yes, I helped Mummy save her too."

"Yes," said the Bush Dreaming Spirits and the Water Dreaming Spirits, "you are all wonderful heroes, because you have saved a little girl – thank you all."

Then many baby turtles came up and said, "we are here to help her too, and we know Bunjee is the hero for saving Bina. He saved her by pulling her out of the water and bringing the blanket for her. And Melee Wallaby and her family saved her from freezing, because they kept her warm with their furry bodies all night."

When they woke, the sun was shining. Bunjee stood up, he stretched his body as dogs do when they wake up from sleeping. He looked at Melee Wallaby and said, "I will go home and get Mum." Melee Wallaby replied, "OK, and we will stay with Bina to keep her warm."

Mum was in the kitchen. She looked out and saw Bunjee running up from the river. She called out, "Poly, Rufus, Molly Dolly, come quickly, Bunjee is home."

We rushed out to meet him. Bunjee saw us and turned around, running back to the river. Poly ran after him and Mum and I followed. We walked as fast as we could, with me watching Mum to make sure she was safe, and didn't fall over.

When we got to where Bunjee stopped, we saw the wallabies lying down close together in a circle. We looked at each other and asked, "where is Bina?"

And then we saw little Bina's head in the middle of the circle – the wallabies didn't move until Mum got there. Melee Wallaby said to the other wallabies, "we must go now, Bina is safe. Bunjee's Mum is here and she will take care of her."

Mum took off her coat, wrapped it around Bina and said, "thank you" to the wallabies. They stood up and watched as Mum carried Bina away. We saw Bina wave to the wallabies, as she hugged Mum. Bunjee grabbed Bina's wet clothes to take them home.

When we got home, Mum called the Police to say we had Bina with us. They called Bina's Mum and the other searchers, and Mum heard on the radio that the Police had said Bina was safe.

Then the Police and other people with big cameras came to our house with Bina's Mum and Dad.

Everyone hugged each other. Bina's Mum and Dad cried as they hugged her and each other.

Bina's Mum asked Bina if she had been frightened. Bina said, "no, because the wallabies and Bunjee told me they would look after me until I was safe with you."

Her Daddy said, "Bina, you mean you can talk to the wallabies?" Bina said, "yes Daddy, they whispered to me in their soft voices, so softly I couldn't hear them sometimes."

The people with cameras asked Mum questions about where she had found Bina.

Mum told them Bunjee had found her, and she also told them that Bina must have fallen into the river, because her clothes were very wet. Mum also said, "Bina must have taken off her wet clothes, and then Bunjee and the wallabies kept her warm all night."

Mum showed everyone the blanket that Bunjee had taken from the shed and had covered Bina with. They saw a lot of wallaby hair and white dog hair from Bunjee on the blanket, and they were puzzled how the blanket got there to cover Bina.

As far as people were concerned, finding Bina was wonderful. They thanked Bunjee and Mum. Television cameras showed Bunjee sitting down and said what a good dog he was, as they showed where Bina had slept.

Bunjee was sad. He said to Poly and me, "look over there, see Melee Wallaby and her family, they are the ones that really saved Bina. But I can't tell anyone they did, because I can't speak Mum's 'people language'."

Bunjee sat down and we looked at Melee Wallaby and her family watching everyone. I wished we could tell people how smart and clever animals like us are.

Fay Nelson O.A.M. & Rufus

These books are dedicated to all my family, wherever they may be today. I have written these books in memory of my Mum (Julia), Dad (Bert Butler Snr), Uncle Romeo, Aunty Mabel, and Granny (Norah Sambo), who raised me on the banks of the Black River, North Queensland, where we lived in dirt floor humpies, hunting and gathering wild food, to supplement our store-bought food.

I also include my children, Tracey, Debbie, and Jeffrey, their children and grandchildren.

My sister, Margaret, and brothers, Noel, Bruce, Bert, Ricko, Gully, and Russell, have all given our family their beautiful children, grandchildren, and great-grandchildren, to maintain our family line.

Mum, Dad, and Granny, taught me to respect myself and all others, our Country, the birds, plants, fish, and animals, and all other living creatures. Each of us has a totemic relationship with them, that lasts a lifetime. They taught me about our Culture and our Lore, which is reflected in each of my books, with the appearances of Bush and Water Spirits.

My pets, Rufus, Bunjee, Poly, and Molly Dolly, gave me precious memories, which I treasure; their presence in my life, helped me through a very difficult time, and continue to help me today, because they show their unconditional love for me, which is why I have written these little books about them.

FAY NELSON O.A.M.

www.ingramcontent.com/pod-product-compliance
Lightning Source LLC
Chambersburg PA
CBHW041105050426

42335CB00046B/129

9 781959 224426